MINISTRY OF MUNITIONS.

Technical Department—Aircraft Production

I.C. 647.

Kingsway,
W.C 2.

L. V. G.

REPORT

ON THE

L.V.G. TWO-SEATER

BIPLANES.

SEPTEMBER, 1918.

J. G. WEIR,

Brigadier-General,

Controller, Technical Department.

The Naval & Military Press Ltd

Published by

The Naval & Military Press Ltd
Unit 10 Ridgewood Industrial Park,
Uckfield, East Sussex,
TN22 5QE England

Tel: +44 (0) 1825 749494
Fax: +44 (0) 1825 765701

www.naval–military–press.com
www.military–genealogy.com

in association with

Imperial War Museums
iwm.org.uk

MINISTRY OF MUNITIONS.

Technical Department—Aircraft Production

I.C. 647.

L. V. G.

Kingsway,
W.C. 2.

REPORT

ON THE

L.V.G. TWO-SEATER
BIPLANES.

SEPTEMBER, 1918.

J. G. WEIR,

Brigadier-General,
Controller, Technical Department.

REPORT

ON THE

L.V.G. Two-Seater Biplanes.

This report is concerned with two L.V.G. biplanes, of which one is of the C.V. type, while the other, a C.VI. type machine, is of later design, embodying certain alterations and improvements. The C.V. machine is allotted G/3BDE/5, and the C.VI. which was brought down near Proven on Aug. 2nd by two S.E. 5's, piloted by Lieuts. Gordon and Gould, is allotted G/2Bde/21.

Any description which follows and is not definitely stated to apply to either model, must be read as appertaining to the C.VI. type.

The C.V. machine was only slightly damaged, and has been put into flying order, but the C.VI. has suffered severely, and it must be stated that on this account the G.A. drawings at the end of this report are not guaranteed to be of absolute accuracy in every respect. The greatest care has, however, been taken in their preparation, and only features of rigging such as dihedral and stagger (besides the tail planes, which are in a very fragmentary condition) are at all doubtful. In matters of detail the drawings are accurate.

Some leading particulars of both machines are given below:—

	C.V. Type.	C.VI. Type.
Weight empty	2,188 lbs.	2,090 lbs.
Total weight	3,141 lbs.	3,036 lbs.
Area of upper wings (with ailerons)...	238.4 sq. ft.	196.0 sq. ft.
Area of lower wings	190.4 sq. ft.	160.0 sq. ft.
Total area of wings	428.8 sq. ft.	356.0 sq. ft.
Loading per sq. ft. of wing surface...	7.3 lbs.	8.5 lbs.
Area of aileron, each	13.6 sq. ft.	11.2 sq. ft.
Area of balance of aileron	.4 sq. ft	0.0 sq. ft.
Area of tail plane	21.6 sq. ft.	28.0 sq. ft.
Area of fin	5.2 sq. ft.	5.2* sq. ft.
Area of rudder	6.8 sq. ft.	6.8* sq. ft.
Area of balance of rudder	.6 sq. ft.	.6* sq. ft.
Area of elevators	20.8 sq. ft.	16.0 sq. ft.
Area of balance of elevator (one)	1.2 sq. ft.	.8 sq. ft.
Total weight per H.P.	13.7 lbs.	13.2 lbs.
Crew	2—Pilot and Observer.	
Armament	1 Spandau and 1 Parabellum gun.	
Engine	230 H.P. Benz.	
Petrol capacity	52½ gals.	52½ gals.

*Assumed same as C.V. type.

Wings.

There are several important differences between the arrangement of main planes of the two models, as will be seen by referring to the G.A. Drawngs.

The wings of the C.V. L.V.G. are without stagger, and are not swept back, but both upper and lower planes are set at a dihedral angle, this being 1 deg. for the upper, and 2 deg. for the lower wings. The lower planes are smaller all round than the upper, and have rounded tips. The upper planes only have ailerons, which are of equal chord throughout their length, and are balanced. These planes also follow what was, until recently, the usual enemy practice, by being joined at their roots to a central cabane. There is, therefore, no horizontal centre section in this aeroplane, except for the 3-ply box (about 4 in. wide), which surrounds the horizontal tube of the cabane. For improving the view, the upper plane is cut away over the pilot's cockpit. Relative to the crankshaft the upper wing has a constant angle of incidence of 5 deg. That of the lower wing is the same, except at the tip, where the angle is washed out to 4 deg., and at the root to 4½ deg.

Both upper and lower wings are attached to the body by the same general means, this being adapted to the particular positions and conditions of each joint. In the case of the upper planes, the cabane has lugs welded to its upper side at both ends. Fig. 1 shows the fitting at the forward end, and the pierced lug on the wing spar (see Fig. 2) fits into the fork. The same type of hinge pin is used for all wing joints, and for the aileron hinges also. It consists of a short length of steel tube, carrying at one end some form of stop, and at its other end a slot in which a short rectangular piece of steel is free to rotate, the steel piece being pivoted at its centre. Thus, when the steel piece is placed parallel to the tube, the whole fitting can be passed through any hole which will accommodate the tube, but when the piece is placed at right angles to the tube axis, the tube cannot be withdrawn through a small hole. A helical spring ensures that the steel piece shall be pressed against the hole, and not be free to slip into the parallel position.

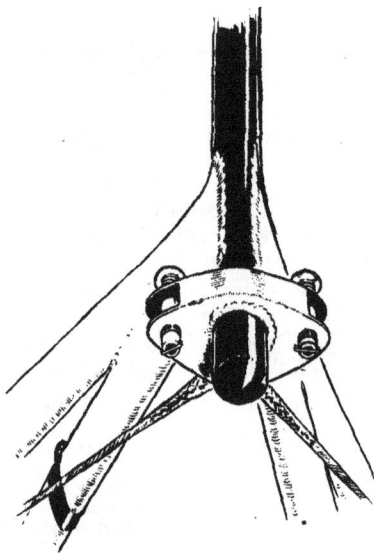

Fig. 1.

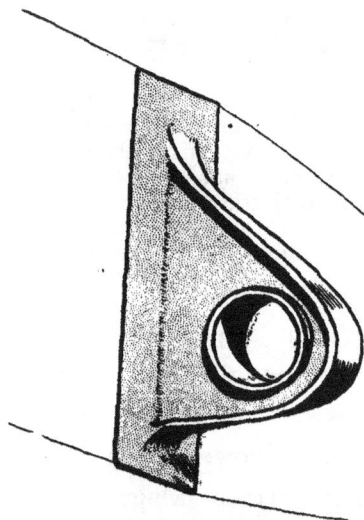

Fig. 2.

The lower wing attachments are very similar, as will be gathered from Figs. 3 and 4, which show respectively the front and rear joints, and this plan has not been changed on the C.VI. type of L.G.V., except that the lug on the wing spar is now fashioned as shown in Fig. 5.

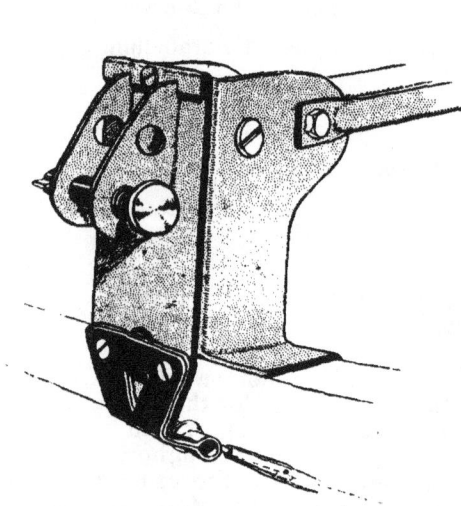

Fig. 3.

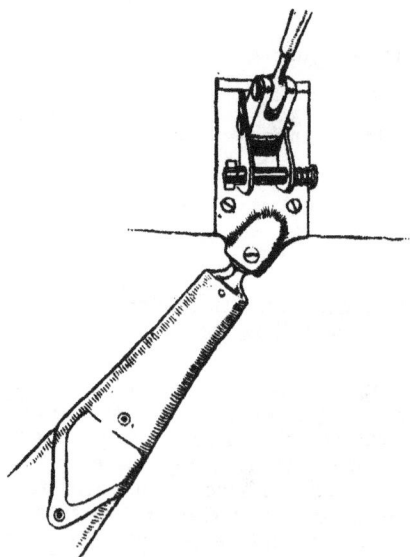

Fig. 4.

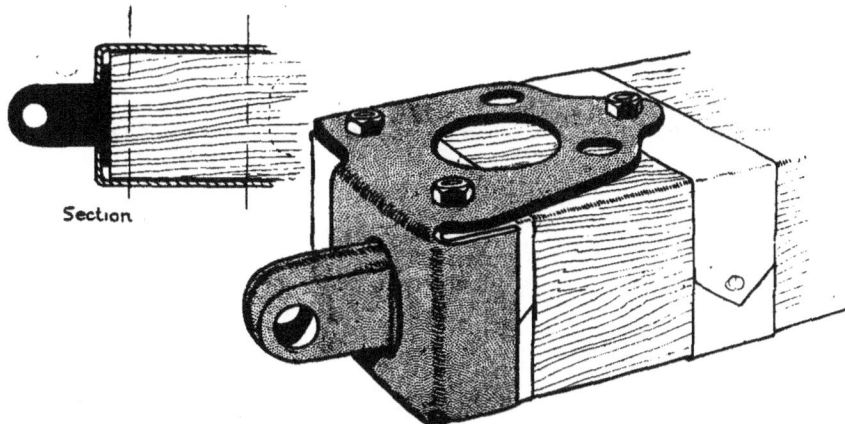

Section

Fig. 5.

In the later model—the C.VI.—the planes are of the same general shape, but important changes are remarked. The radiator has been moved from the position it occupied on the C.V. (see G.A. Drawings), and is now built into the horizontal centre section. It is, of course, common German practice to build the radiator into the upper plane, and such a position is not incompatible with the cabane type of centre section strutting. This is particularly true when—as is the case in the L.V.G.—a service petrol tank is supported by the upper plane, and can be made to balance the radiator. It is clear, therefore, that the alteration in design from the cabane system to the centre section system has not been made solely to accommodate the radiator.

So far as may be judged from the machine in its present condition, the C.VI. has a positive stagger of 10 in., and both upper and lower planes have a similar dihedral angle, viz., 1 deg. Ailerons are still fitted to the upper plane only, but are not balanced in this model. The upper and lower wing sections of the C.VI. model are shown in Fig. 6, and Fig. 7 gives the C.VI. upper wing section with the R.A.F. 14 section superimposed. The R.A.F. 14 section is dotted.

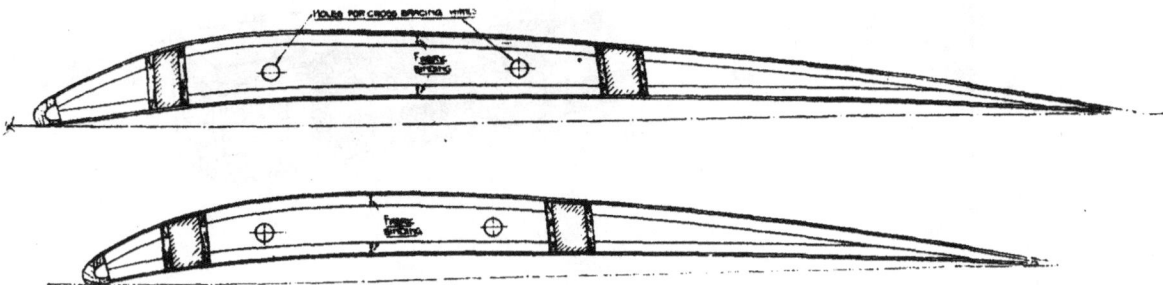

Fig. 6.

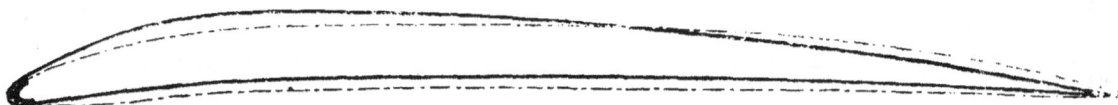

Fig. 7.

Wing Construction.

(These details were all noticed in the C.VI. machine, as in the earlier type the planes are still covered with fabric.)

Both front and rear spars are of the box type, and wrapped with fabric. Sections drawn to scale are given in Fig. 8, but these drawings do not show internal construction, as the spars have not yet been divided.

The overall height and width of each spar, taken respectively parallel and perpendicular to the vertical walls, are:—Upper plane, front spar, height $3\frac{1}{4}$ in., width $1\frac{7}{16}$ in.; rear spar, height 3 in., width $1\frac{5}{16}$ in. Lower plane, rear spar, height 3 in., width $1\frac{1}{16}$ in.; front spar, height $2\frac{7}{8}$ in., width $1\frac{11}{16}$ in.

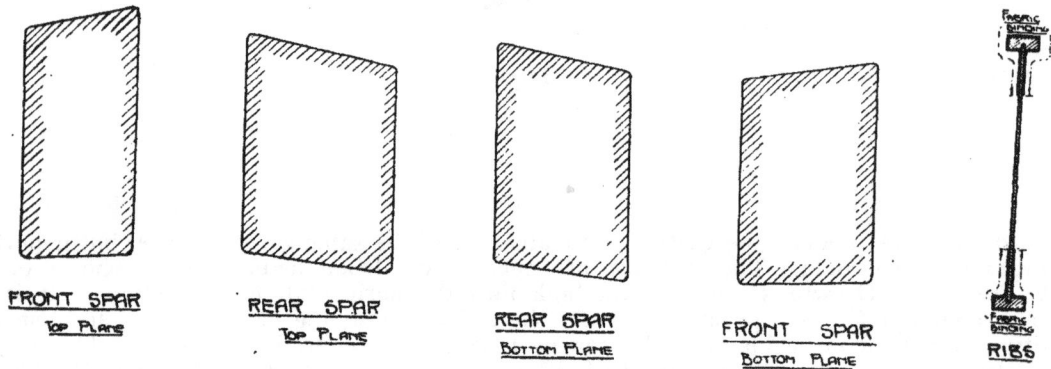

FRONT SPAR
Top Plane

REAR SPAR
Top Plane

REAR SPAR
Bottom Plane

FRONT SPAR
Bottom Plane

RIBS

Fig. 8.

It has been possible to draw a section of the front spar of the C.V. machine, and the result is given in Fig. 9. There is every reason to believe that all the other spars of the L.V.G. are of similar construction. Fig. 10 shows a crude but effective method of repairing a broken spar. The repair was carried out by the enemy, probably in the field.

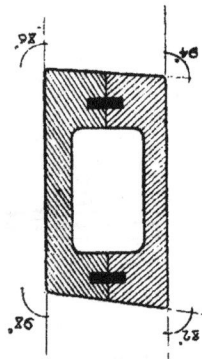

Fig. 9.

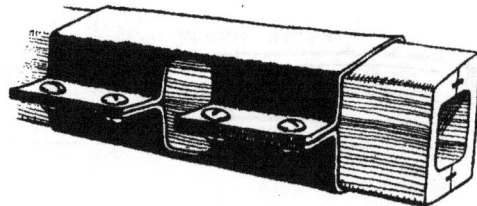

Fig. 10.

The leading edge is of the customary C section, and is followed at 7 in. interval by the front spar. The space between the two spars—$25\frac{3}{4}$ in. wide—is braced with cables and piano wire, and contains four ash compression struts of I section, which are simply butted into sockets obviously intended to carry steel tubes. (These compression struts are steel in the C.V. model.) The distance from the rear spar to the wire trailing edge is 2 ft. $6\frac{3}{8}$ in. The ribs, of which a section is shown, are of the usual type, and are spaced at intervals of $16\frac{3}{4}$ in., centre to centre. They are unlightened. Equally between them are placed two false ribs—mere strips of wood let into the leading edge and tacked to the spars. These false ribs have floating ends $7\frac{1}{2}$ in. behind the rear spar.

The construction of the lower plane does not differ from that of the upper plane just described, except that the false ribs are not found in it.

Ailerons.

The ailerons of the L.V.G. no longer possess the peculiar step in the trailing edge that has for so long been associated with the design, and the ailerons are rather different in the two types. The C.V. model has ailerons which are balanced, while those of the C.VI. are not. The respective areas are given on the first page of the report. With regard to the constructional features, only those of the later type can be described. The whole construction is of wood, with the exception of the aileron lever, a sketch of which is given (Fig. 11). This is of the usual curved type in the C.V. machine (see Fig. 12), but is made to serve as a rib also in the C.VI. type. The wooden ribs, together with the wood leading and trailing edges, form a structure which is very light. Both machines have the ailerons hinged to a false spar some distance behind the rear spar, and the hinges are all of the type that has already been described in connection with the wing attachments (see Fig. 13).

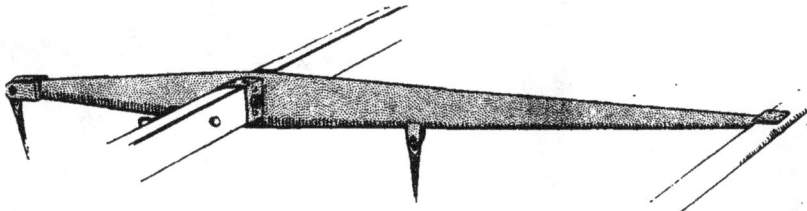

Fig. 11.

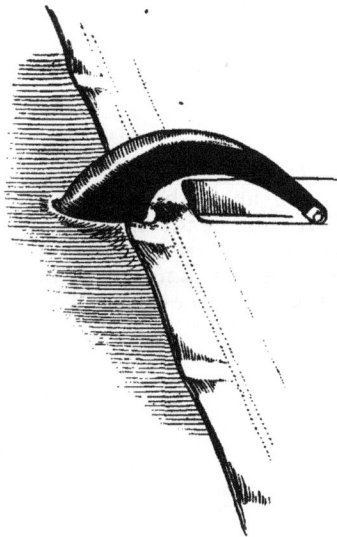

Fig. 12.

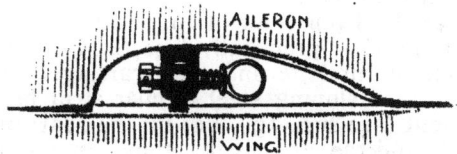

Fig. 13.

Struts.

The L.V.G. is one of the few enemy aeroplanes that employ interplane struts of wood. They are of the shape shown in Fig. 14, and are of streamline section ($2\frac{1}{4}$ in. $\times$ $1\frac{9}{16}$ in.), slightly hollowed out for lightening purposes. Fabric is wrapped round the strut in three places, and the form of the strut sockets is made clear in the sketch (Fig. 14), which shows one of the C.V. struts.

The types of strut socket employed in the C.VI. machine is shown in Fig. 15, while Fig. 16 shows how the strut is attached to the spar. The socket is held in place on the strut by simply inserting a suitable length of steel tube through a drilled hole in socket and strut and rivetting over the ends.

As has already been mentioned, the centre section struts are different in the two types. In the C.V. machine the cabane, the shape of which is made clear by the G.A. Drawings, is made of streamline steel tubing. This has been changed, and the C.VI. model has parallel centre section struts of wood, which are like the letter N when seen from the port side. Fig. 17 shows the joint between the spar of the centre section and the strut. The unusual arrangement of the cross-bracing of this centre section should be noticed in the front view, General Arrangement Drawings.

Fig. 14.

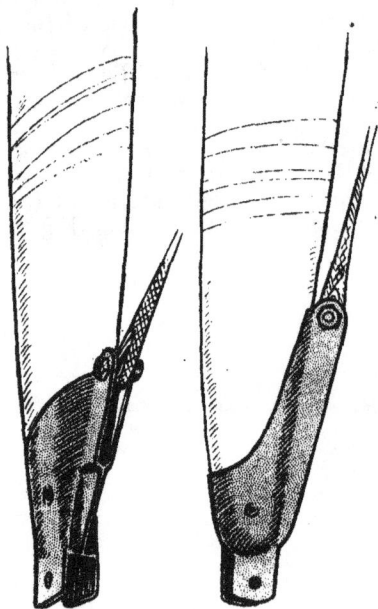

Fig. 15.

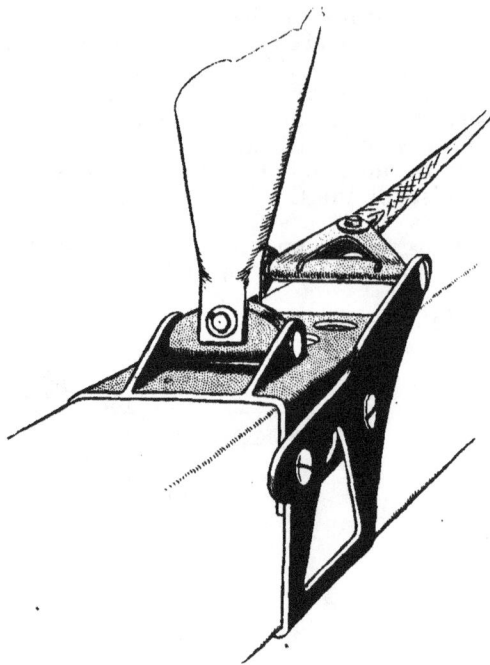

Fig. 16.

The line of the front limb of the N is carried on by the third fuselage bulkhead, and finishes at the front joint of fuselage and undercarriage. The angle between the rear two limbs of the N is practically bisected by the line of the fifth bulkhead, which finishes at the rear joint of fuselage and undercarriage. This is shown by a diagram, Fig. 18. The C.V. machine has a sloping steel tubular strut between engine bearer and rear undercarriage attachment (see Fig. 19), but by the rearrangement of bulkheads the necessity for this has vanished, and the strut is not found in the later model.

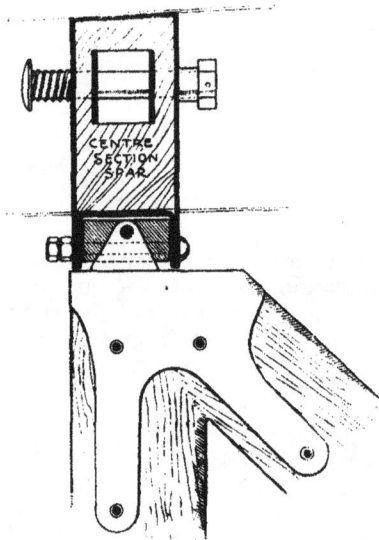

Fig. 17.

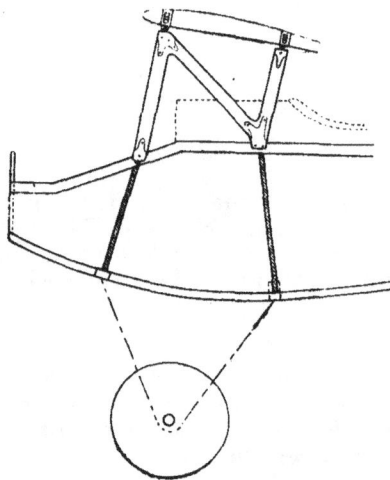

Fig. 18.

Fuselage.

The earlier types of L.V.G. had bodies built on the cross-braced girder system. Both the machines described possess the same type of fuselage, totally different from the girder system, viz., a framework of bulkheads and longerons, covered with a thin layer of 3-ply, and totally without wire bracing. Fig. 20 gives the number and shapes of the bulkhead in the C.V. machine, and incidentally reveals the shape of the fuselage. The C.VI. type has generally the same arrangement, but the third and fifth bulkhead are no longer vertical in this model, and the tail part of the body has been strengthened by the insertion of another cross piece.

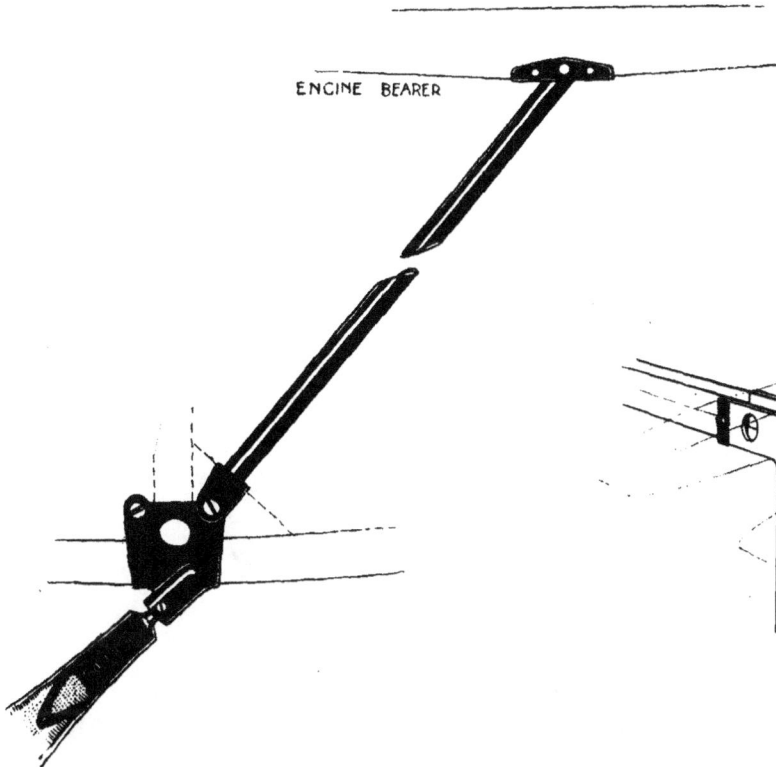

ENGINE BEARER

Fig. 19.

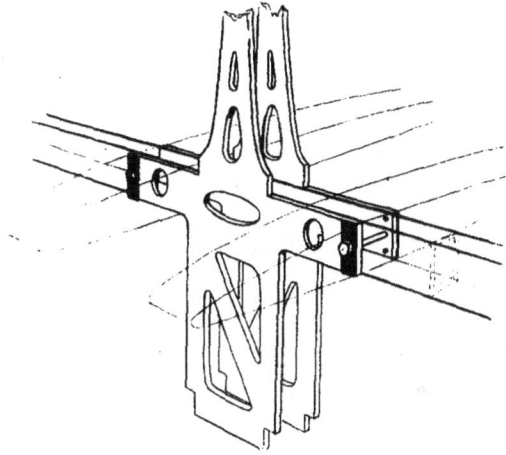

Fig. 21.

Although the fuselage of the L.V.G. biplane ends in a vertical wedge, the provision of a centre section for the tail plane gives a cruciform appearance to this part. This is shown clearly by Fig. 21, where the two sides of the tail plane centre section are drawn in thin lines. The 3-ply covering to the fuselage rounds off the joint of body and tail plane in the neat way that is found in so many German aeroplanes. (See Fig. 22).

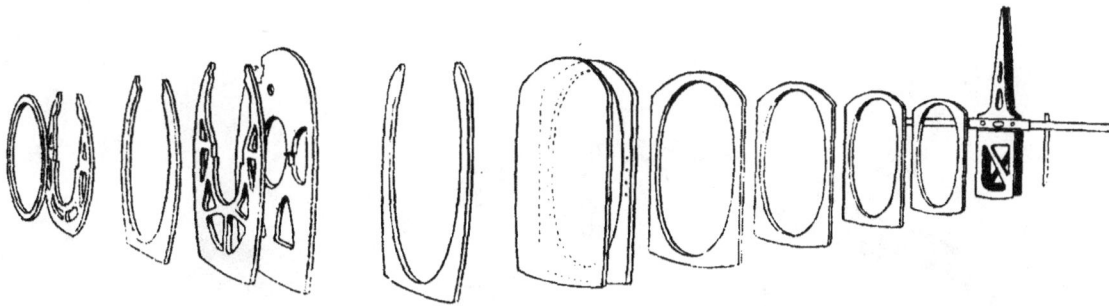

Fig. 20.

Tail.

The shape of the fixed tail planes is shown in the G.A. Drawings. The main box spar (see dotted section in Fig. 21) passes right through the body. The rear spar, to which the elevators are hinged, is of rectangular section wood, hollowed on its rear face to take the steel tube which serves as the elevator spar. The tail is so badly damaged that detailed analysis is impossible, but the fixed tail planes are of wooden construction, with the usual ribs and semicircular leading edge. It will be noticed that the tail plane is not set parallel to the crankshaft line, but is raised through an angle of 5 deg., and it has a symmetrical streamline section.

The elevator, which is balanced and undivided in both models, is a welded structure of light steel tubing, and presents no unusual feature. There is a small protecting horn provided on the tail plane, to prevent damage to the corner of the balanced portion of the elevator—Fig. 23 gives a clear idea of this example of thoroughness.

Fig. 22.

Fig. 23.

The tail skids are both of the same general type as that of the Pfalz Scout, i.e., the member is entirely exposed, and does not project into the fuselage. It is of ash, and the upper end is so shaped as to avoid the necessity for any metal link or fitting. Both machines also have a small triangular fin on the underside of the fuselage which serves the double purpose of providing fin area and of adapting the shape of the fuselage to the slope required for the tail skid. (See Fig. 22.)

It will be seen from the sketch (Fig. 24) that the skid of the C.V. machine carries a four-leaved flat spring bolted a little to the rear of the pivot. In the later model this has been discarded. The shape of the lower triangular fin also differs slightly—that of the C.VI. has been simplified and strengthened. The workmanship of the sheet steel angle piece on the C.VI. machine gives one the impression that it is a "squadron fitting." It is of fairly heavy gauge, and may have replaced a weaker part fitted by the manufacturer.

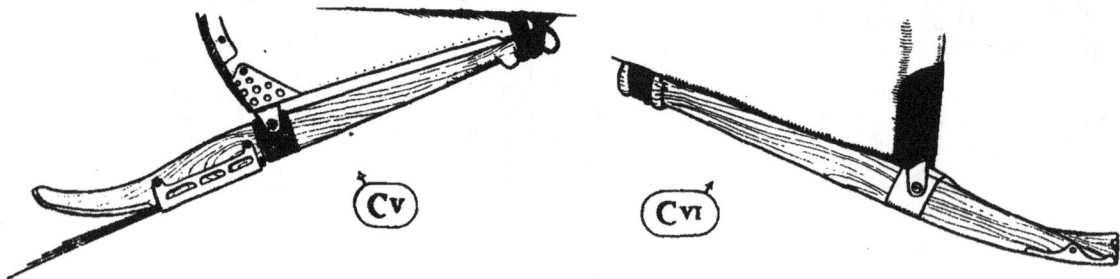

Fig. 24.

Undercarriage.

The landing gears of both machines are similar, and in general arrangement conform to the practice that is now practically standard. The vee struts are of streamline section, and constructed of fabric-covered wood. The practice of using wood for undercarriage struts is, of course, unusual in enemy machines, but is in conformity with the other struts —interplane and centre section—on this machine.

The major and minor axes of cross section of one of the front struts (and all four, front and rear, are of equal dimensions) are respectively $2\frac{9}{32}$ in. and $4\frac{7}{8}$ in.

The upper and lower extremities are capped with steel sockets, which allow of attachment to the fuselage at the upper extremities and at the lower ends serve to connect the two limbs of the vee, and are provided with accommodation for the shock absorber. Figs. 25 and 26 show respectively the component parts of the attachment to the fuselage, and the socket at the lower part of the vee. From Fig. 25 it will be noticed that the ball at the head of the strut beds into a hemispherical socket attached to the fuselage. The lower half of the ball articulates with a curved surface on the ferrule, and the ferrule next slipped over attachment. In assembling this joint—and this is a matter of seconds only—the ball is first passed through the opening provided on the ferrule, and the ferrule next slipped over the body lug and pinned in place. All four body attachments are of this type in the C.VI. machines, but in the C.V. model the joint was made by simply pinning the ball to its socket, without the refinement of a ferrule.

The shock absorber is of the coil spring type, with three small diameter springs lying side by side, as indicated in Fig. 26. A loop of cable limits the amount of axle travel, and between the lower extremities of the vees is a steel compression tube, of $1\frac{1}{2}$ in. O.D., and behind this lies the axle, which is encased in a 3-ply fairing. It will be noticed that the compression tube is not included in the fairing, and when the axle is raised as the machine lands, the fairing travels with the axle. This method allows of good accessibility to these components, but is not quite so good an arrangement from the streamline point of view as the common method of allowing the axle to lift out of a fixed fairing.

The schedule of principal weights, given at the end of this report, is of considerable interest as regards the undercarriage.

The wheels are 810 × 125, and the track 6 ft. 7 in. The cross bracing does not start from either front or rear fuselage attachments, but from the front spar joint on the fuselage.

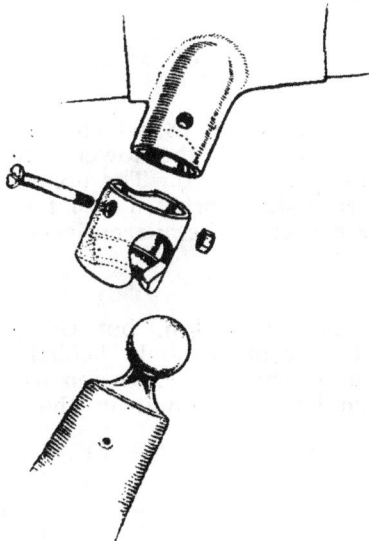

Fig. 25.

Fig. 26.

Controls.

As is the case throughout the design, the controls of the two aeroplanes are generally similar, but differ in detail. In the C.V. machine, the control lever, at the head of which is the usual two-handed grip, operates two rocking shafts which are perpendicular to one another. The transverse tube, which actuates the elevators, is cranked in the middle and supported on four brackets, marked a, b, c, and d, in Fig. 27, which act as bearings. To the middle point is pinned the front half of the jaw which is found on the bottom of the control lever. This pin A, always points directly to the centre of the pin B, which passes through the rear half of the jaw and is itself always exactly in line with the bearing of the transverse shaft. This somewhat complicated arrangement allows the transverse shaft to be rotated round axis a, b, B, c, d, and at the same time permits the other shaft to rock on its own bearings. A simple contracting band brake controlled by a Bowden lever and cable serves to lock the elevator controls in any desired position. This brake is found in both types.

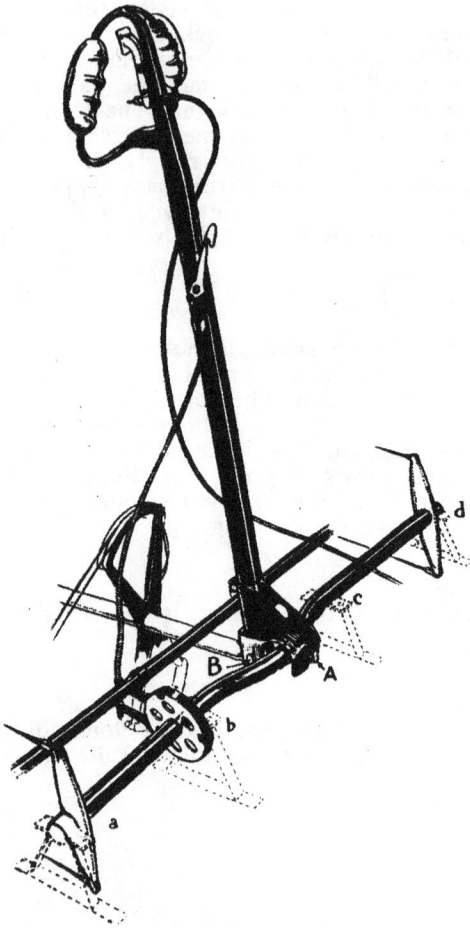

Fig. 27.

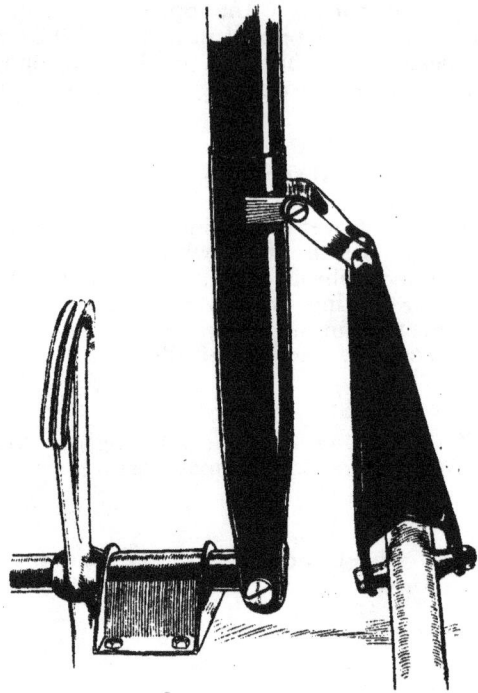

Fig. 28.

The C.VI. controls are rather different. and are shown in Fig. 28, which clearly explains their operation. The naked aileron control cables pass through the lower wing near the rear spar, and run over the aluminium pulleys illustrated in Fig. 29. The upper extremities of these cables are attached to the welded control lever which works in a slot in the upper plane. The differences between the two types in the matter of the aileron lever has already been commented upon.

The rudder bars of the two types are of the same general design, but the problem of leading the cables round the base of the large petrol tank immediately behind the rudder bar, is solved in different ways. In the later type, a semicircular extension to the rudder bar avoids the necessity for the two extra pulleys and bearings found in the C.V. type. Reference to Fig. 31 will make this point clear.

Fig. 29.

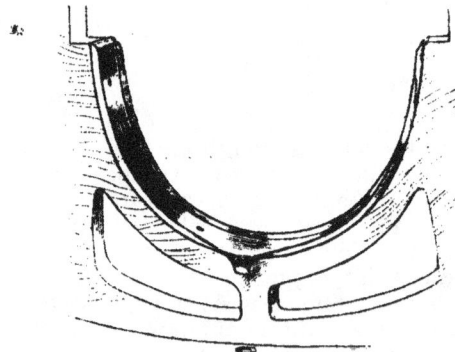

Fig. 30.

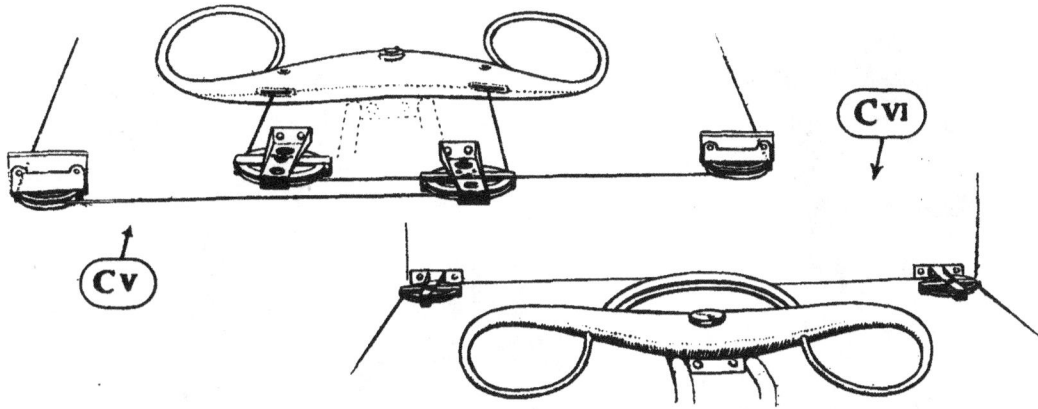

Fig. 31.

Engine Mounting and Control.

The 230 H.P. Benz engine is mounted on wooden bearers of rectangular section, 1⅝ in. wide and 3¼ in. deep, supported on the cross bulkheads found in the front of the fuselage.

In the C.V. machine there is a steel tubular strut on each side which is in compression between the rear portion of the engine bearer and the front undercarriage joint (see Fig. 19). As has already been mentioned, the rearrangement of the fuselage bulkheads allows this strut to be dispensed with in the C.VI. model.

The throttle lever is of the familiar ratchet-quadrant type, and in the C.V. machine there is no interconnected throttle lever on the control stick. Although the C.VI. control lever is missing, it is fairly certain that this is true of this type also. Those bulkheads which are likely to receive oil drippings from the crankcase are protected by aluminium strips employed in the manner shown in Fig. 30.

Oil and Petrol Systems.

Both machines have a main petrol tank under the pilot's seat, and a gravity tank attached to the upper plane. In the C.V. machine this tank is placed on the upper surface of the port plane, alongside the narrow centre section. The later type has the tank beneath the port upper plane, as will be noticed from the scale drawings. In this case the filler passes through the plane, and has the cap on the plane's upper surface.

The C.VI. main tank has a capacity of 47 gallons, and the gravity tank a capacity of 5½ gallons, thus giving a total petrol capacity of 52½ gallons. There is a hand petrol pump which allows the pilot to fill the gravity tank from the main tank, and an engine petrol pump which draws fuel from the main tank and passes it on under pressure to the small cylindrical compartment of the main tank, whence it flows to the carburettor. This is, of course, the usual Benz system, and has been fully reported upon.

The exhaust pipes are of welded sheet steel, and are carried higher than is usual in the C.VI. model (see Fig. 32).

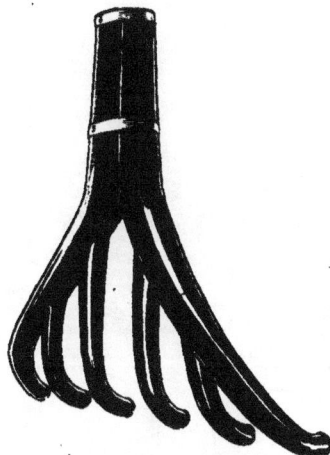

Fig. 32.

Fig. 33.

Radiator.

The positions respectively occupied by the radiators of the two models are quite different, though both are in conformity with enemy practice. Reference to the scale drawings will make it clear that the C.V. radiator is supported in front of the leading edge of the upper plane on struts clamped to the cabane, while that of the C.VI. occupies the middle part of the centre section and is flush with the curvature. The construction also differs. The vertical (C.V.) radiator is composed of flat vertical films, which are crimped and set "staggered" so that their appearance is similar to that of a honeycomb radiator. The C.V. type has the usual oval section brass tubes running perpendicular to the chord of the wing. Fig. 33 gives a sketch of the earlier radiator, and of its supports. The shutters work on different systems, as will be noticed from the sketches. The vertical shutter of the C.V. machine is of the roller blind type, with cables which operate positively, one to unroll and the other to roll up the blind. This shutter puts out of action approximately one third of the radiator area. The C.VI. shutter effect is obtained by moving a handle which alters the slope of nine parallel hinged flaps, as illustrated in Fig. 34.

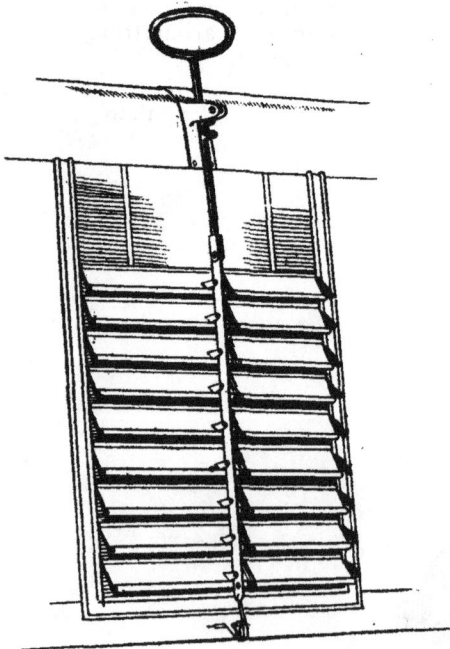

Fig. 34.

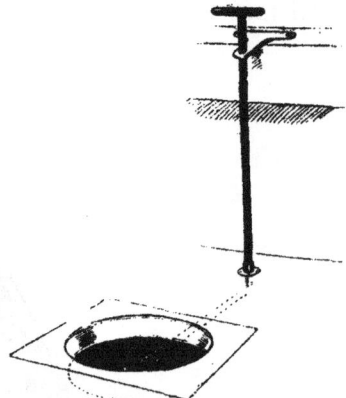

Fig. 35.

Instruments.

The pilot's cockpit is not provided with a dashboard, but the instruments are distributed chiefly on the left-hand side of the pilot. They comprise the usual Bosch starting magneto and key switch; an oil-pressure gauge calibrated to 4 kg. per sq. cm.; a petrol-pressure gauge to .5 kg. per sq. cm.; a Maximall petrol gauge to the main tank, a grease pump, and throttle and ignition levers of the usual type.

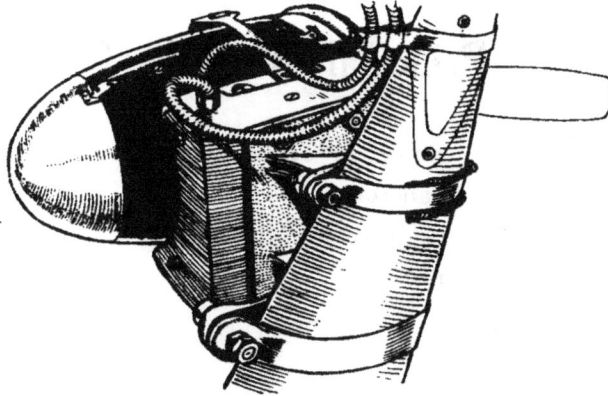

Fig. 36.

The observer's cockpits of both machines are provided with circular camera holes in the flooring, and each hole is fitted with an aluminium cover, but these covers are manipulated differently. The aperture of the C.V. machine is about 9 in. in diameter, and the type of cover is clearly shown in Fig. 35. That of the C.VI. model is 12 in. in diameter, and is covered simply by an aluminium sheet which slides in parallel grooves outside the fuselage. The C.VI. biplane was fitted with a complete wireless outfit when captured, but of the internal fittings only the aerial and reel remain, and these are entirely standard. The current was obtained from a dynamo attached to the undercarriage strut, which is still *in situ*, though its propeller is missing. This dynamo is shown in Fig. 36.

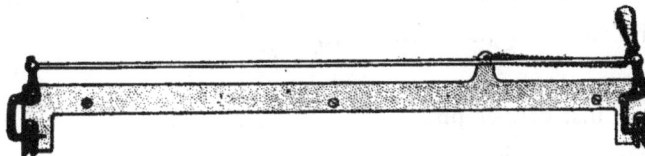

Fig. 37.

The fitting shown in Fig. 37 was found on the starboard side of the C.V. machine; and is obviously a release for some light object. Its precise function is unknown. Fig. 38 shows the C.VI. gun ring, and it will be noticed that the padded clip is not in its usual vertical position.

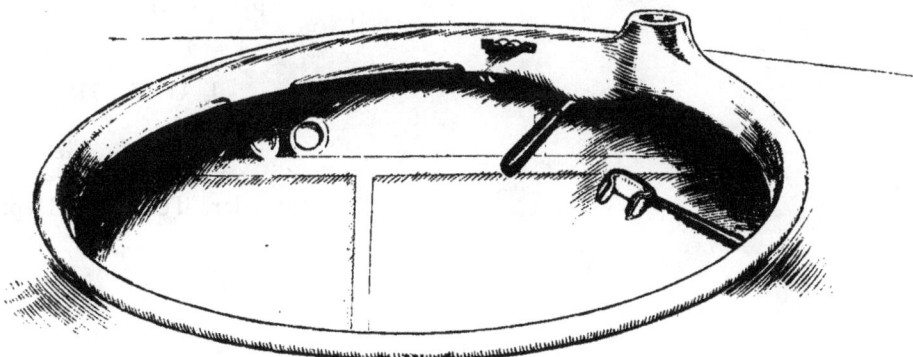

Fig. 38.

Fabric and Dope.

The usual printed fabric with a design of coloured polygons is used, and nothing regarding fabric or painting calls for comment.

Schedule of Principal Weights (C.VI. Type.)

	lbs.	ozs.
Fuselage, without undercarriage, engine, or centre section	440	0
Lower wing, covered complete (no ailerons)...	76	12
Upper wing, covered complete, (with ailerons)	85	4
Centre section without struts or cable	64	0
Centre section N strut	5	8
Interplane strut, each	3	11
Aileron, covered, each	8	4
Balanced elevator, covered, complete in one piece	14	8
Undercarriage, comprising :—		
2 Vees, bare	29	1
2 Wheels, with tyres	55	8
2 Axle caps, with pins		6
2 Shock absorber bobbins	1	4
2 Shock absorbers	17	6
Axle and fairing	23	2½
Compression tube in front of axle	3	0
2 Bracing wires, with strainers	2	0
4 Ferrules		10
Undercarriage, complete	132	5½
Tail skid, bare	4	6
Brass oil tank, with 20 ins. copper pipe	9	7
Ammunition magazine (aluminium)	5	0
Exhaust pipe	16	4
Spinner	2	9
Dynamo, without propeller	23	12

Both of these aeroplanes are at present at the Enemy Aircraft View Room, Islington. Passes may be obtained on application to:—The Controller, Technical Dept., Ap.D. (L.), Central House, Kingsway, W.C. 2.

Ap.D. (L.)

J. G. WEIR,

Brig.-Gen.,

Controller, Technical Department.

SEMI-PLAN VIEW.

SIDE VIEW.

FRONT VIEW.

NOTE.—These photographs are of a C.V. type L.V.G.

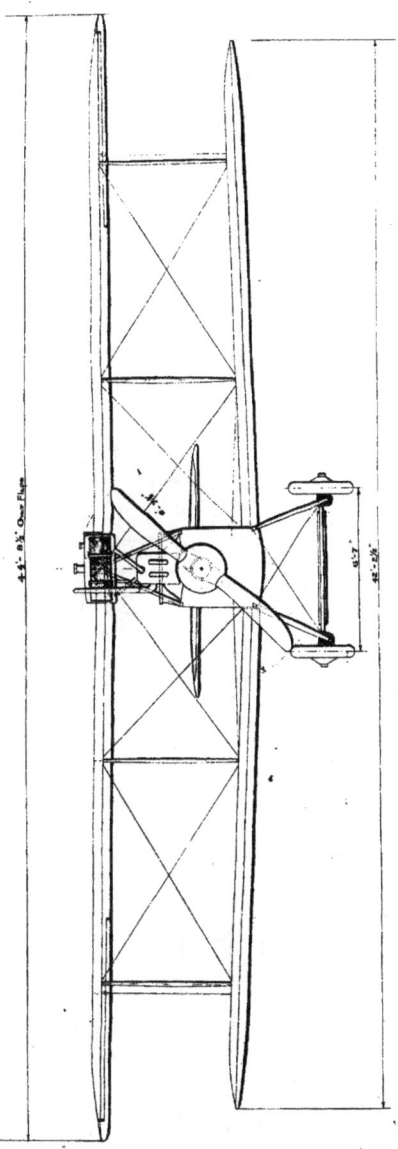

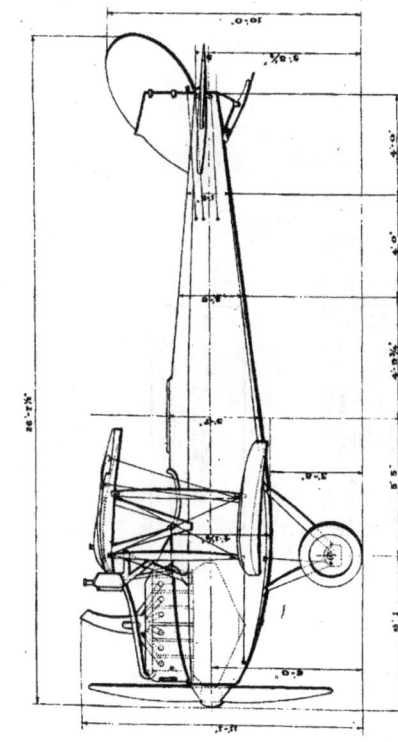

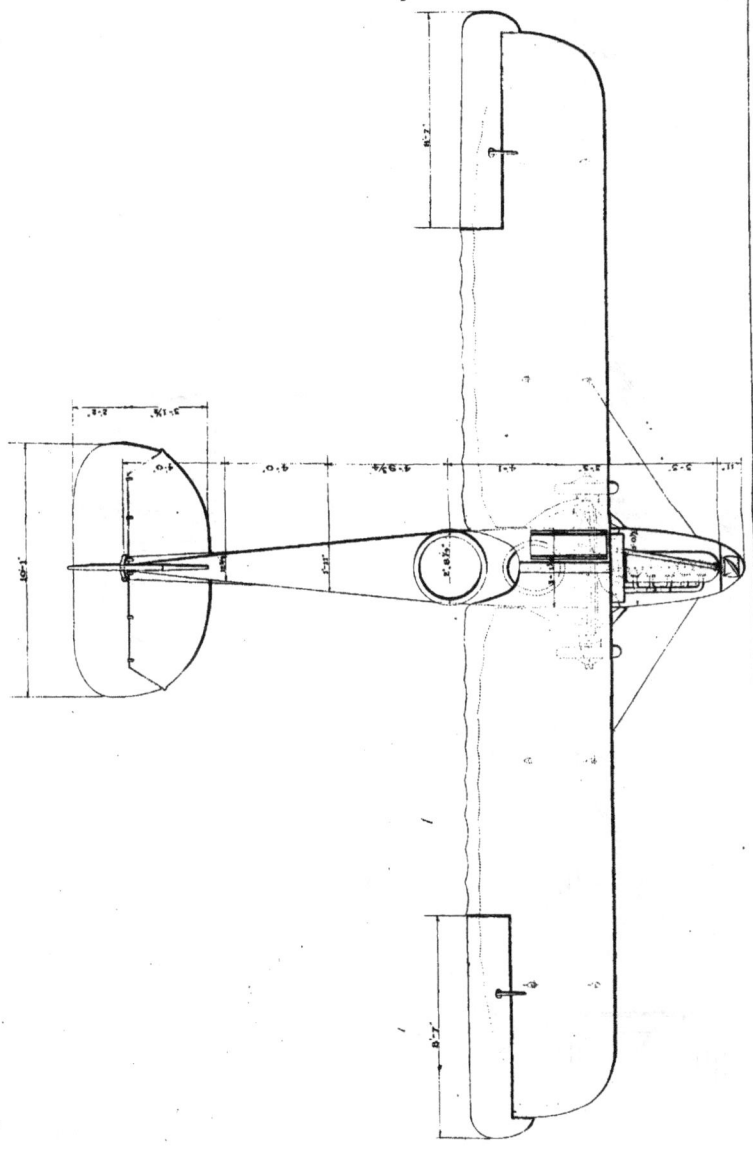

Span of Top Plane (overall)	42'-6½"
Span of Lower Plane	42'-9½"
Length Overall	26'-7½"
Gap of Inner Struts	5'-8¼"
Gap at Outer Struts	5'-6½"
Chord of Top Plane	5'-8½"
Chord of Lower Plane	5'-3"
Angle of Incidence	3°
Dihedral Angle (Top Plane)	1°
Dihedral Angle (Lower Plane)	2°

L.V.G.
C.V Type Biplane

D.D.G.E. T.5 R.738 1900 10/43

L. V. G.
C VI TYPE

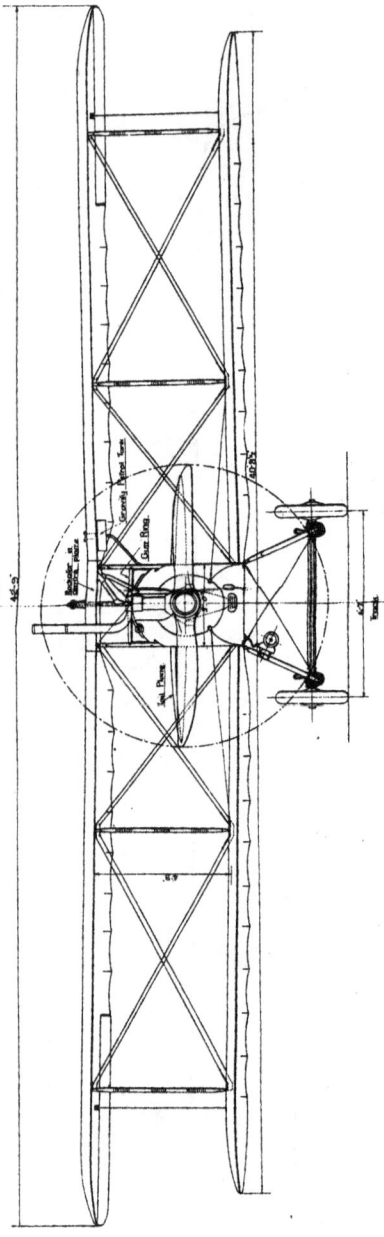

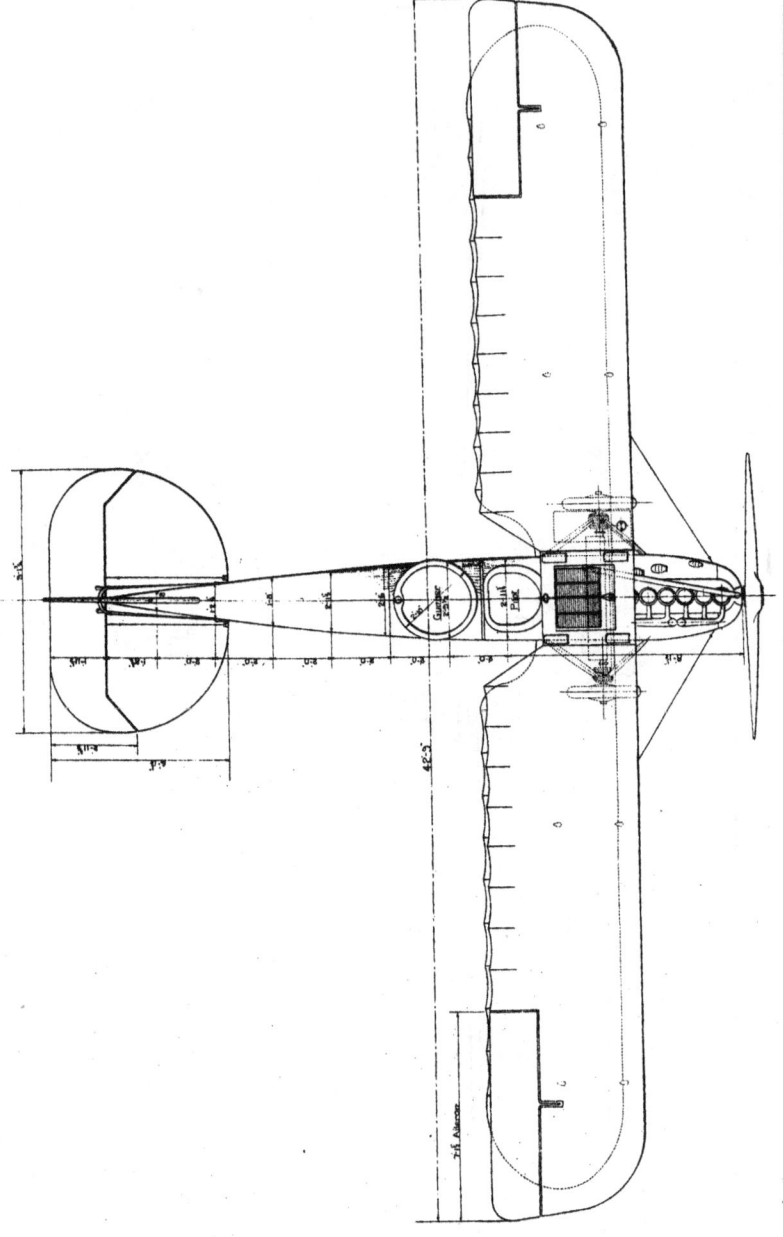

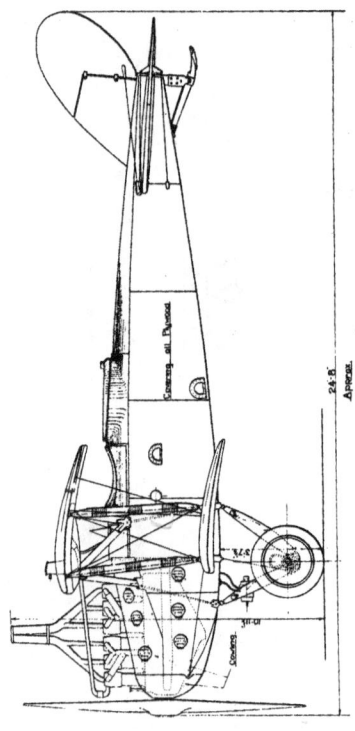

Span Top Plane	42'·9
Span Bottom Plane	40'·8½
Length overall (approx.)	24'·8
Gap	4'·9
Chord Top Plane	5'·3
Chord Bottom Plane	4'·7½
Angle of Incidence Top Plane	6½°
Angle of Incidence Bottom Plane	5°
Dihedral Angle both planes	1°

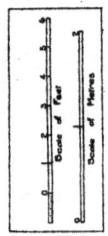

Scale of Feet

Scale of Metres

The C.VI. L.V.G. Biplane.

The C.VI. L.V.G. Biplane.

The C.VI. L.V.G. Biplane.

The C.VI. L.V.G. Biplane.